ZPL

Allosaurus

By Joanne Mattern
Illustrations by Jeffrey Mangiat

Reading Consultant: Susan Nations, M.Ed.,
author/literacy coach/consultant in literacy development
Science Consultant: Darla Zelenitsky, Ph.D.,
Assistant Professor of Dinosaur Paleontology at the University of Calgary, Canada

WEEKLY READER®
PUBLISHING

Please visit our web site at www.garethstevens.com.
For a free color catalog describing our list of high-quality books,
call 1-800-542-2595 (USA) or 1-800-387-3178 (Canada).
Our fax: 1-877-542-2596

Library of Congress Cataloging-in-Publication Data

Mattern, Joanne, 1963–
    Allosaurus / by Joanne Mattern ; illustrations by Jeffrey Mangiat.
      p. cm. — (Let's read about dinosaurs)
    Includes bibliographical references and index.
    ISBN-10: 0-8368-9414-6   ISBN-13: 978-0-8368-9414-1 (lib. bdg.)
    ISBN-10: 0-8368-9418-9   ISBN-13: 978-0-8368-9418-9 (softcover)
    1. Allosaurus—Juvenile literature. I. Mangiat, Jeffrey, ill. II. Title.
QE862.S3M3319   2009
567.912—dc22   2008024774

This edition first published in 2009 by
Weekly Reader® Books
An Imprint of Gareth Stevens Publishing
1 Reader's Digest Road
Pleasantville, NY 10570-7000 USA

Executive Managing Editor: Lisa M. Herrington
Creative Director: Lisa Donovan
Senior Editor: Barbara Bakowski
Art Director: Ken Crossland
Publisher: Keith Garton

Printed in the United States of America

1 2 3 4 5 6 7 8 9 10 09 08

Table of Contents

Boldface words appear in the glossary.

A Different Lizard

Meet Allosaurus (al-loh-SAWR-us). Allosaurus was a big dinosaur. It lived in North America.

Allosaurus was about as long as three small cars. It was as tall as an elephant.

Allosaurus's name means "different lizard." Its back bones were different from the bones of other known dinosaurs.

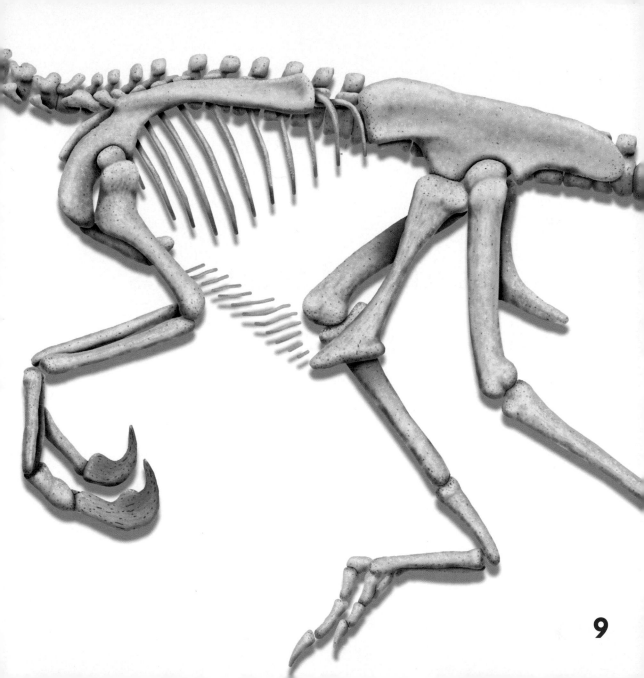

9

Allosaurus had short arms and a long, heavy tail. It ran on long back legs.

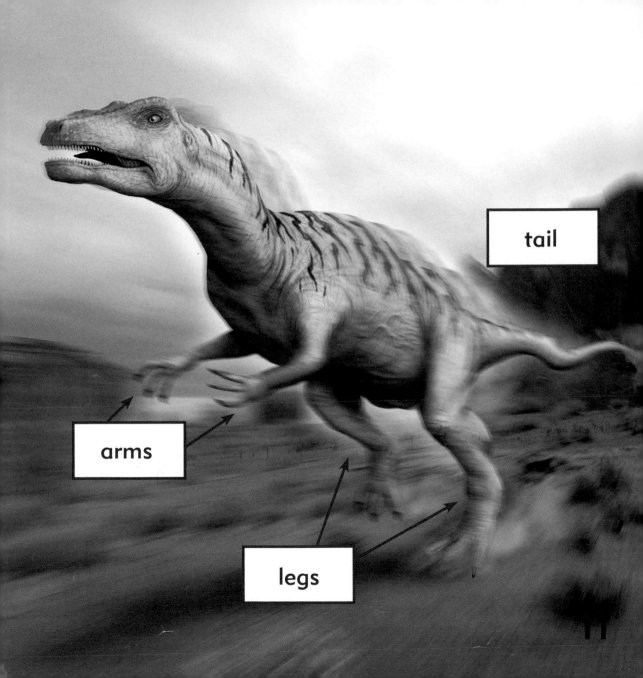

tail

arms

legs

Claws and Jaws

Allosaurus had three
fingers on each arm.
Each finger had a long,
sharp claw.

claws

Allosaurus ate meat. It hunted other dinosaurs. Allosaurus used its long claws to grab **prey**.

Allosaurus had strong jaws with long, sharp teeth. The teeth curved backward. They were just right for ripping into prey.

A Peek at the Past

Scientists found the first Allosaurus **skeleton** about 130 years ago. They have found many Allosaurus bones in western North America.

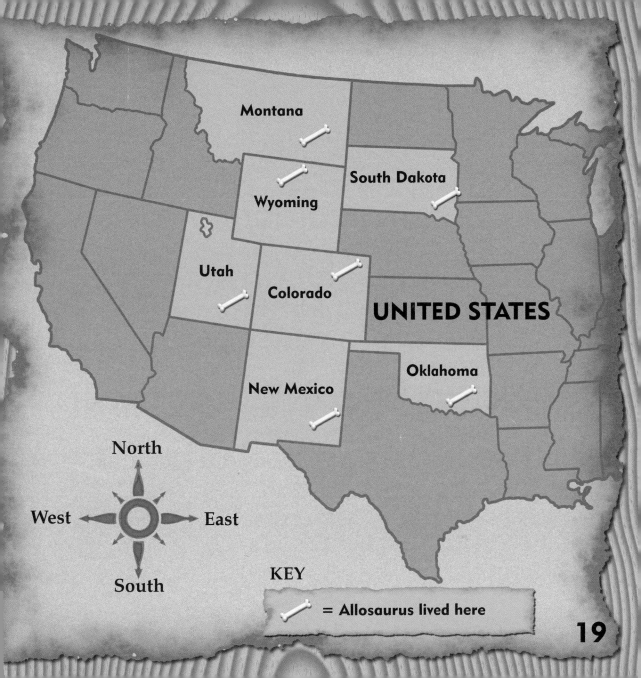

Montana

Wyoming

South Dakota

Utah

Colorado

UNITED STATES

New Mexico

Oklahoma

North

West ← → East

South

KEY

= Allosaurus lived here

Allosaurus died out long ago. Today, we can see its skeleton in **museums**. Skeletons help us learn about Allosaurus and its world.

ALLOSAURUS

Glossary

museums: places where people can see interesting objects on display

prey: animals that are hunted and eaten by other animals

skeleton: the bones that make up an animal's body

For More Information

Books

Dinosaur Claws and Crests. Prehistoric Creatures (series). Joanne Mattern (Gareth Stevens Publishing, 2006)

Strange Lizard: The Adventure of Allosaurus. Dinosaur World (series). Michael Dahl (Picture Window Books, 2005)

Web Sites

Dinosaurs for Kids: Allosaurus
www.kidsdinos.com/dinosaurs-for-children .php?dinosaur=Allosaurus
This site has fun facts, illustrations, a map, and a time line.

Zoom Dinosaurs: Allosaurus
www.enchantedlearning.com/subjects/dinosaurs/ dinos/Allosaurus
Find more facts about Allosaurus and see its skeleton.

Index

About the Author

Joanne Mattern has written more than 250 books for children. She has written about weird animals, sports, world cities, dinosaurs, and many other subjects. Joanne also works in her local library. She lives in New York state with her husband, four children, and assorted pets. She enjoys animals, music, reading, hiking, and visiting schools to talk about her books.